JUSTICE FOR ROMEO

SIOBHAN HODGE

Other publications by Siobhan Hodge

POETRY

Picking up the Pieces

JUSTICE FOR ROMEO

SIOBHAN HODGE

CorditeBooks

First printed in 2018
by Cordite Publishing Inc.

PO Box 393
Carlton South 3053
Victoria, Australia
cordite.org.au | corditebooks.org.au

National Library of Australia
Cataloguing-in-Publication:

Hodge, Siobhan
Justice for Romeo
978-0-6480568-0-5 paperback
I. Title.
A821.3

Poetry set in Bembo 10 / 14
Cover design by Zoë Sadokierski
Text design by Kent MacCarter and Zoë Sadokierski
Printed and bound by McPherson's Printing, Maryborough, Victoria.

 Cordite Publishing Inc. thanks Penelope Goodes, Dennis Haskell and Siobhan Hodge for their input during the production and editing of this book.

10 9 8 7 6 5 4 3 2 1

For Gina and River, among many, many others.

A successful teacher must have a thorough knowledge of his pupils. The rider should know his horse physically as well as mentally. He should have not only a thorough knowledge of the horse's anatomy and of the functions of his joints and muscles but also be able to understand his feelings and anticipate his reactions.

—ALOIS PODHAJSKY

It is best to let the horse go his way, and pretend it is yours. There is no secret so close as that between a rider and his horse.

—R S SURTEES

CONTENTS

PREFACE xi

INTRODUCTION xiii

AUTOPSY

Happy Valley Turnover 3
Autopsy of a Race Horse 4
Racing Colours 6
October Horse 8
Melbourne Cup 2014 9

THE ORCHARD

Darker Horse 13
Farewell 14
Stubbs's 15
Stone Horses 16

OLD PARTISANS

Trophy Cabinet 23
The Hack Show 24
Brand Name 25
Circular Logic 26

MY FOE'S DEBT

You Know? 31
The Volta 32
In the Pines 34
Bone Binds 41
Wrong Lead 44

FICTIONS OF LEGS

Bodylines 49
Draw Reins 50
Buyer Beware 51
Half-Pass 52
Slipped 53

BY ANY OTHER NAME

Zebra 57
Przewalski's Pelts 59
Sable Island Horses 60
Horse Latitudes 61
Lake Gregory Horses 62

JUSTICE FOR ROMEO

Treatment 67
Fracture 68
Theory for Everything and Nothing 70

IN MEMORIAM

Sold On 75
Rinjani 76
For Gina 77

NOTES 81

ACKNOWLEDGEMENTS 83

PREFACE

Horses have been intrinsic to much of human history. Their connection to human activities has always been dualistic, but also beset with ironies. Equine connections to human activities have always been dualistic: horses are linked with both deities and domestic drudgery; lauded as symbols of freedom and subservience; relied upon as a vital means of transportation and agricultural labour, or considered a luxurious indulgence. In Europe from the sixteenth century onwards, artistic and literary representations of horses started a tendency towards the anthropomorphic, moving away from dead-eyed mechanical portraits. In the eighteenth century, romanticised portrayals of horses began a steady rise to primacy. Today, horses maintain a liminal position enjoyed by few animals: they are not quite pets, but not quite livestock. They are still working animals, but also easily replaced by machines or human athletes. Scientific knowledge of how to best raise, train and manage horses is flourishing, yet long cultures of anecdotes and training theories, grounded in highly subjective and often questionably founded interpretations of equine behaviour, reign supreme in many circles.

Who is Romeo? He was not my horse. In life he was a symptom of all that is wrong with industrial-scale equine production. He fell victim to human interests in as many ways as it was possible to fall. Well-meaning ignorance is as dangerous as malice. Amongst horse people, this is also often called love.

INTRODUCTION

Justice for Romeo, as a title, will seem both accurate and misleading for most readers; this is a book decidedly concerned with justice, and Siobhan Hodge's sense of ethical responsibility pervades the poems. Hodge's book includes as epigraph the exchange between Romeo and a servant in Act I, Scene ii of the most famous love story of all time; the servant asks, 'I pray, can you read any thing you see?', to which Romeo replies, 'Ay, if I know the letters and the language.' This epigraph has significance for the whole poetry collection, since Shakespeare's play is as much about blind hatred as it is about love; Romeo's reading the letter immediately after this exchange begins the tragedy.

However, we are misreading when we rush to identify Hodge's title with Shakespeare's character. For Hodge's Romeo is, or was, a horse, and this collection is the first Australian book of poetry entirely given to horses and human interactions with them. Horses have been domesticated since 4000 BCE and the book is centrally concerned with the way that domestication occurs and is maintained.

The opening epigraph instructs, 'The rider should know his horse physically as well as mentally … to understand his feelings and anticipate his reactions'. Hodge's searching and heartfelt meditations show that this is true but glib; she does attempt empathy in the poems, but recognises that sympathy is as far as she, or any human, can go. Horses feel, think, see and react differently to us, and *Justice for Romeo* is an appeal to respect their independence and right to being. The second epigraph says, 'It is best to let the horse go his way, and pretend it is yours'. We live in a period when the human capacity for empathy and sympathy with the other, not only with animals but immigrants, refugees and the planet itself, seems in short supply; this only serves to emphasise the importance of what these poems are attempting.

While Hodge's writing is spare and dispassionate in tone, the poems leave us no doubt about her view of the injustices done to horses: for money through racing, for work and their treatment as machines, for war, 'teeth … poised / for battle', and sometimes even for art. Hodge's own stance contrasts with a history of human arrogance but she is a skilful enough writer that her judgements are embedded in the poems.

Poetry, with its power of sensory evocation, is a fine vehicle for conveying such thought and experience, and Hodge's poetic forms range from Shakespearean sonnet to prose poem. When riding, she and the horse are very much part of nature but when, for example in the poem 'In the Pines', she and the horse fall or approach a poisonous dugite snake, nature is not sentimentalised. These are poems which show not just knowledge and admiration for extraordinary creatures – that is, horses, not people – but a mature acceptance of the world as it is. Even Hodge's accidents with horses recounted in 'Bone Binds' are evoked without bitterness as 'aerial / lift' with 'Air kinder / than ground'.

Hodge's poems give the horses' 'throttled tongues' some voice, eradicating a 'curriculum of silence' but in *our* letters and language, so that the poems tell us about human imagination, fear, wish for power and concern with beauty. She has a greater variety of rhythms than *The Man from Snowy River*, so ride along with her: 'in this mess we're together'.

—Dennis Haskell

AUTOPSY

No philosophers so thoroughly
comprehend us as dogs and horses.

—HERMAN MELVILLE

Happy Valley Turnover

American alfalfa, fresh
off the jet, arrives
for a visiting
sprinter
in the barracks.

Soybean starches
ulcered bellies,
oats and lucerne
for horses ushered
to another day's racing.

Withers judder
in humid clumps,
remembering
seasons in uneasy
halogen nights.

Eyes turn
to Kowloon skyline
under lock
from stall to killing pen,
now harried up the ramp.

Seychelles broke fast,
Sicilian Storm no
breeder,
along the outside
we have another
Ferdinand.

Imported hay
exchanged
for spent bodies
on the morning truck.
Punters park elsewhere.

Autopsy of a Race Horse

To measure the draw–
strength of tendons
skin is peeled.

Disable nerve points

Chipped bones can now
be removed, spurs
filed,

Evidence of lung scarring

hindsight reigns
in fluid pockets
ruptured on factory floor.

Fine-boned   *Always trouble*

Steaming counterweight
of intestines tugged
to gauge internals.

Gut ulcers far back   *Advanced*

Engine failure
scrap,
too easy to pull

Four years   *Gelding*

the bullet,
restart an engine
on redundant model.

Looks like a bleeder

No more complex
than the wirings
of these bones.

Throat surgery here

Remember placement,
re-pin pastiche
of natural selection,

Evidence of laminitis

mount on
a rack, suspended
on hollow hooves

Not much of a looker

another prototype
emptied and strung up
behind closed doors.

Racing Colours

Red dirt races, weekend dive again
to wilting finish
and small cheques.

Lean bay bodies measure all distance,
universal guess
of each length.

Anonymity of agouti,
tacked silks turn shoulders,
neck or hip.

Rotational cut frozen upon
scapula, or seared
to profile.

Patina of sweat reads effort more
cleanly than whip glance,
shuttering

each propulsion. In no other sport
is the athlete struck
for effort.

Facial blur crosses the line, snap up
win by a whisker
or tipped hoof –

each skinned hide a penalty blow,
drawn by eye outside
court contempt

for blood bubbling on lips from lung,
but not leg, nor bruise
heading home.

Plastic snap grades colour behind rail,
impartial tarps hide
the fallen.

It's a tough game, some say, with no runner
available
for comment.

October Horse

Equus October was an ancient Roman sacrifice to Mars, where the winning horse of a chariot team would be ceremonially speared and displayed.

Right hand leads
and spear is cast
into spent chest.

The victor's body
will be bronzed
and staked

than to erect
statue, race,
or film

one leg will start,
it's hardly surgical.
Remember the heart

superannuate
these winnings.
Another Ruffian

Your head is wreathed,
tugged and torn
by the crowd.

by the punters' tent.
No better way
to forget

after. There,
no sense in feeling
these leads –

and forget the bones,
sinews and flexors
that could never

or Go For Wand to shield
until the race is earning
and we count the dead.

Melbourne Cup 2014

Fascinators squared
on each television
the year humidity struck
                                        an alarming froth.
                                        Stoop to scratch.
                                        We need the best.
Champagne bubbles
on heaving flanks,
unfamiliar names spill
                                        some coddled child.
                                        It's held close,
                                        port to paddock and will never want
for love. Adoration is newspaper
thin, stronger prayer
than tarpaulin – spread
for two this time
                                        when said. *Show a little respect,*
                                        they're not all like that,
                                        accidents happen.
Another accident then. Two bodies
Manjimup wine and punters
cool behind white screens.
No need to scare the children,
they love to run.
More than anything,
he died earning his promise.
Projection beams
from both sides. There's money in anatomy,
but no steel. Another break, another loss
to feed and house.
                                        Shrouds count
                                        cheques, not the dead, and we're set.

THE ORCHARD

We kept him until he died ... and sat with him
during the long last minutes when a horse
comes closest to seeming human.

—CJJ MULLEN

Darker Horse

Slicing earth, you write
along ground
past eye shot, away
from fence and lead.

Iced air droops, I feel
each breath, wet slap,
four beats a tribute,
directives I may not read.

Advance or retreat, I
want you to see me,
a snipped membrane.
You melt through copper.

Each streak signs you,
each strike and lift, no joint
contract. Solar flip,
my unmasked mentor.

I wonder at your upward
glance, why your thrown head
turns to see, but prefer
its remains, a mystery to me.

Farewell

for Caroline Norton

Precious body flung to earth,
that spine did not bear
you any ill or more
intent than the force that brought
you down
but still you wore
its skin. You may not
mount again – meek steed,
casting that beast adrift
to send you home, gold
lost over the side.
You speak of loss
and hear,
more perfect than sinew
can suspend,
but no touch guides
that fall. Shattered back.
A less fond hand
more feared
than desert paths, far reaches
towards you. Sent away,
your exile wreathes the grave
more thickly than mirage.
White-lipped boy, lost
underground, gripes of memory,
of the rush and thud,
back down to earth
unstrung. Alone in the field,
he watched the sky continue
and you remain
holding the reins. You
might chafe in factories.
No head for freedom,
mouth bared, you slipped away
after what apples do.

Stubbs's

The first map was drawn
over territory hung
from the rafters.
That remote cottage must
have worn death
like a curtain, limp legs wired
and backs arched as though
caught in a dance. Youth
to fill your space
between canvas and cadaver.
You learned every slice,
peeling sinews back with tender
strokes. Every hair in place
and noted. Gracious in your
gruesome labours, museums
note. Each jugular drained,
veins puffed with molten
wax. Your soft intrusion
fills every part. Each tender
touch frames eyes peeled.
You will know each
close layer. Every private space
must be nicked and noted.
For eighteen months you walked
between the bodies, swinging bellies
yielding to every push. The
mouths are stitched
in charcoal. Whistlejacket attacked
his own wide arrogance,
posed on chalk feet. Your lion
frightens another. Deep plates
hold anatomical precision,
served to royal house. No
crowds at the scene,
but each painting rolls
stolen eyes.

Stone Horses

Each horse in this frieze is unique in temperament and personality. No horse is a duplicate of any other; the arrangement of head, neck, body, and limbs differs, even if only slightly.

—Mary B Moore, 'Horse Care as Depicted on Greek Vases before 400 B.C.'

I

On the frieze
plaster has peeled
across one flank
and buttock

open-book
nicked stone
feels parched
as meat.

All along the wall
stern forelegs bend
towards lined bellies, flush
and veined in plaster.

More frozen steeds
arching for
the best hands
lucre can pass.

II

Your face is familiar.
Pale walls at
the university, and here
you're also mounted:

stunned eye stretched bare,
plum nostrils and mouth
peeled back, reined
line to breakage.

They have no ear
for you here, either –
eyelids hollow as your plaster
body, lower set

in Perth. I itch
to translate distance
palming forehead, but will
not provoke ejection.

III

Each pony
strung
up, erect
lip curls

necks bulge with
indignant whispers,
museum rush
of waterline

manes missing,
Centauric body,
smooth agency
of traded plaster.

IV

These teeth are poised
for battle.
Hock arcs to tuck,
chipped hooves
to strike. To fight is no
foreign thought,
all known equine bickering
pales before
organised iron intent
to maim. Each leap and snap
for display
rerouted, ridden down
no path
any horse could hope
to follow.

OLD PARTISANS

And indeed, a horse who bears himself proudly is a thing of such beauty and astonishment that he attracts the eyes of all beholders. No one will tire of looking at him as long as he will display himself in his splendour.

—XENOPHON

Trophy Cabinet

Blooded projections claim
the wall. Each rose-edged
photo crowned like stags
with mouths ajar.

Famed breeder
in retirement,
though each horse still poses
neatly boxed for display.

She leads me down
the mouldering hall,
Too many ribbons to keep,
you know, I gave them away.

Among the gilt
an uncured hoof silts mantel
wood, dust lacquering
rank over memory.

Pride of float
still placed in braids,
Baiardo's tail wears roses
thick as millstones.

She pets trophies,
recalls each one
mounted. Photos
name each frozen face,

grease-lidded eyes
swivel under candlepower.
A legacy of tombs.
Her horses buried inside and out.

The Hack Show

This is not a normal horse reaction to a human and clearly denotes abuse.
—Section 9.6.A, The Arabian Horse Society of Australia

You can meet your face
reflected in the mawkish

painted flanks. Rugged
like vintage cars in summer.

Heads froth with powder
bent for judgement.

Centre gaze trims
to size thick splits

of buttered meat,
patched skeletal fissures

and maudlin eyes
sunk under resin.

Hooves snap carnival
smart on chains, tongue lolls

flashing false tail seams
all screened from judgement.

Spur flinch. Dye leaves
foamy residue beneath

what's smooth and white,
smearing jackboot calves

pinned to ribs, and clothing
blue intent.

Brand Name

The smoke today
is wet with you,
folded trap of fence
and wire under down,
moulded sign leaks flame
one press: clean through.

A name, your shoulder,
dripped on hip or
smeared along the neck
will show more clearly
than the secret stain
scrawled upon your lip.

Tidy hyphens so encase
the skin now flat and dead.
Each point will pin
you here. Go. Move along
the next body. Will it remain
in code? Set and bled.

Circular Logic

Silence is not acoustic. It is a change of mind, a turning around.

—John Cage

Hear that default
radii repeat:
turn him in
a circle's circle, as it were,
to build the brakes
or muscles'
tempo
rhythm
or cadence. A unit
suspended in circular

thinking. The horse's body
is a wheel   we just have to get
it turning the right way.
Millennia breeds
indifference,
to hours
laps
strides
to ulcers. Rifling for something
that may never.

The German training scale
seats straightness so far
along its education plan,
insensate and trapped
percolating
my track   my time   my goal
a horse
worrying at imperfections
of design.

MY FOE'S DEBT

The horse you get off is not the same as the horse you got on. It is your job as a rider to ensure that as often as possible, the change is for the better.

—CORMAC McCARTHY

You Know?

You can get diamanté-studded
spurs, you know, delicate
pins to complete the picture,
lining the shop like children
and their toys. I've never worn
the urge, don't you think,
I've never carried a whip and plied
an unresponsive flank, each slap
to echo through my hands. It's mine,
I wear it cold. Coloured ropes
and halters, rainbow cheek-pieces
bound to twisted snaffles,
pink crops and children's bats, the
swatter even shaped like a hand,
the facsimile would mean
no less than the assault itself.
There is no way you know
to get a horse to move
if it doesn't want to you know
there's no way a tiny person
could hurt an animal
that large with such a tiny stick
you know they have it thick
in the skin, you know there's nothing
one little smack to move
them, there's nothing more to that
than we have tools

and our purposes don't let them
tell you it's cruel
I know, and have done,
and am done.
All sense has gotten us
somewhere
we should have known.

The Volta

Thirteen again, watching
the dust settle. A rangy grey
has ducked out of line,
drawn thin
in sand set soft,
it may not have
been at all.
I remember
no slight that widely
provoked your ire.
Primed between a line
and rod, I am only dull
witness to your assault.

The rope is chucked, hiss
belly-deep.
Hooves circulate
a half-moon gaze
that cannot lift.
Wilted mane
too long to braid
gummed flat
with sweat. And stilt
his fearful pace,
how it stirs
your crop, antenna in electrical

storm now a snake,
squat and spoiling.

Just try it, mate.

Most children recoiled,
your shoulders slick in rigid
certainty.

Show'im who's boss

or some such grouse, inked
by time, I have not seen
more tenderness than mane.
I see him stilled,
lacquered lean by sweat.
The whip
didn't speak, your face alone
struck him down, each trembled ear
swivelling inward. Not this
battery of energy,
crackling, shorting out,
pinioned between shed
and eye that would not yield
infinitesimal ground
for error.

I will
no more codify your violence
than that damned horse could.

In the Pines

This forest was no
natural fact, blown
book-keeping
pace with tankers,
cover the cash
flip and cycle
of the seasons.

We follow half-tyre markers,

of dunes under needles,
pine cones and the fat
resins of summer,
ripped offal of bin liners
sleek on the sand

we skirt each car
that creeps along
the firing lines.

Take stock,
access points: chipped lime
and lazy poles, they'll hold
a flow of cars, but
any pony can clamber
over leaning barriers,

we slip and step
in silence.

Parallel lines:
kangaroos don't use
the same trails,
while dialect lift of weeds
nags wattle. Twist of
burr upon your fetlocks,
dust settles on grids
of ageing trunks. Root rot
or run-off? Gnangara shift
to Wanneroo, out and up
the map is stroked

in long slashes of track
and tread, scrub cedes space
to each new pine.
A history that agonises
under new revision.
Names are numbers
billed and broken
with every debate.
No ownership can   I claim
and like others
                                        I steer
                                        between fissures
                                        and we make another mark.

Old certainty
of place: who can stay?
This pine tree land,
no man's land – only women
                                    I've seen
their paths
making along the margins.
Hiding from the strikes,
swinging solace under leaden branches.
Colour blind
after dark, but not before
                                    I will not
entertain the murmurs
each forgotten debt
a score out in this sideways forest
tips and splitting the land
in savage new histories,
given back, then snatched away.
The pines have drained
its force with vengeance.
Here   we find wreckage,
the legacy of losing

and refuse,
thrown out
but waiting:
abandoned fridges
honeycombed with rust,
an affront
of shredded plastic, warm
bleaching toys and
garden trimmings
tossed   our track
we're never unexpected.
One day, they will return
to sneer and shake heads,
but not today.
Still,   I slow you for fear
of glass under sand;
vanity of control
cannot prevent your
assault, but would pin
its place. Blood on sand
or sap?

I can almost feel.

Hooves trim verge
between kangaroo-paw
and torched Ford morbidity.
Picked exoskeleton
of a gutted tent, shucked barrels
and toothless mower are human
punctuation in this abattoir line
of waiting trees.
But there is life here. Dugites stir
from afternoon
glare, and you smell
their aches, each flinch on dumped paint
cans.   I turn my head on,

catch fumes
while you read another page.
Does the sap rise
inside these trees
huddled in a meal
for death and paint the sand
in gaudy sheets when
the chainsaws come again?

We're not welcome,
those days.

Sawdust breath and scrabbling troughs
of subterrenes dragged away at night,
witnessed by emu, roo, some rat.
The snakes unfurl
to each dropped needle
and four-wheel exit,
gateways seeded and unbent,
waiting to recoil. The heat
is patience, wanting, all
at once. Your head
combs to check, then moves us both along.

I follow,

let you set the pace, cut through
these memories of breath,
and wonder where
the water waits.

We pick up a trot
in unquiet dunes.

Beyond the rows
each step sinks
further in the firebreak.
Curve of nostrils,
mathematics of sweat is gilt,
intent phosphoric as a path
under orbs of spiders' web.

Why do we persist? Our lines

are fed on fear each time
we whip the road.

Collective space in shadow,
your black coat nips
encroaching sunset,
throw the lens astray
at lines we do not own
in fallen trees. Soaked
needles, lost maps and each
breath shared,
your heart beneath   my legs,
and ribs security
how my hands
needn't stray
from your mouth. Connection variant
I am the crutch
and cross you bear.
Fingers write apologies
in stiff orbits
about your aching neck.
Each stride is another episode
for curvature.
You press   I am
here, losing pace
as you make the metres
sweep away
in steps of fallen trees, soaked
needles and lost maps.

Pines thin and an emu
looms level. Lean-spined, you jump,
will never read these
bodies. Inclination of eyes
and you start
up, head higher than

skeletal reference.
You fell to earth
on the same soil,
no
home for you   or I, but only one
has transaction of space.
                                                                        We gut
                                                                        the scrub in sharp strokes

but it's all too much:
reins fracture
the final stroke – now,
the fall.

Wrinkled body on ash

                                                    you forget me soon

enough. Widowed rider
out before dark
loses sight faster
than path: how far back?

Home is organisation
of space in lines
that feed and flutter
with fragments. Dust is thickening
between my lungs.

Dark horse at dusk
flatline, speed-drunk
shucking the wrongness
of it all. She would not
claim this place. Hooves
repel her moons in sand
and night, it slips about me
as I walk.

Imported trees

and pilfered land no
flight to agency ripped
from bloodied hands.
Another was lost here
for four days, found strung
and swollen, mouthing
northern borders.
Each foot bursts indignant,
coordinating tracks
in strides her own
downward fixation impact
and the pines they hiss eviction.

A satellite
out of gravity,
its pull, I read
stranger lights
under the reddish spray
of trodden sap:

stride – object,
artefact, untelling.

Leading me to strainer post ribs,
gnawed by sand the clawing
of dragged pines.   I see her snagged
along the fence line.
Wide eyes wait for reason,
fear is alcoholic.
Reclaim in soft
consent, we are the linked.
The pines, the pines'
exhalation rank
and warning dead
in name alone. We take
up the path and do not go out again.

Bone Binds

The head and face sustain 20% of horse-related injuries … The age at which most injury occurred is less than 21 years … No horse is a safe horse; some are safer than others but the horse is a potentially lethal animal. Prevention of accidents and injuries is dependent upon using knowledge previously obtained from studying horse activities.

—D BIXBY-HAMMETT, W H BROOKS, 'Common injuries in horseback riding. A review'.

I – Lucky

The first was payment
only due
in parts – a chip.
Dislocation barely held
the contact
a moment, then
dissolution, swept
and dropped outside.
Debris is removed
like teeth through wire.

The other party,
pay not yet tendered,
left by the clean, sharp
strokes of an engine
reset. Watching
the extraction, those crescents
cycled out and my father's
legs sprung in, cyclic
under halogen lights.
The sand framed the snap,
hospital drive lost to sleep.

II – Riverdance

The second was aerial
lift, burst banks
on dried lake bed. Interruption
chemical, no intent
to surface. Air kinder
than ground,
pale ears all caught
in light as the sand
came roaring back.
Snapped neck
and no excuses.

Upon return, only sky
and my father's arms.
Each step was heavier
than the fall. Voices
and braces, ambulance
intrigue and the question
of where she'd gotten –
I remember the date
but couldn't recall it –
cause for concern
committed to memory.

III – Gina

The third time
was my own design.
Argument struck
on terms I did not
take. Ejection prompt
and flat. Dark horse
denial, dull dismount
put out right hand first –
no cushion for arrogance,
dropped to sand
and gutted trees.

She had no reason to stay,
exit stage front
neatly over gate. No need
for hand to hold or hinder –
this was not her dilemma,
shun the scene.
Sand under nails,
walk was clean, finger flagged
and trailing. I made my own way
home, and still can't fault
the terms for severance.

Wrong Lead

It was a bit of a shock to discover that in fact they can't see when their heads are pulled in like that. And it's really rather a scary thought that people are riding around so much these days with their horses like that.

—ALISON HARMAN

All along the division
lines of lateral flex
and bend, cite
ivory technicality
to select where
each foot lands.

Learn by rote what
route to take – text
to trophy – count
circles in tangent points,
weigh submission
in throttled tongues.

Bearing each academic
thrust of angle,
conception of arc
and swing are payment
for service rendered,
broke and boarded.

My nudge of heel to rib
is precise science, connect hock
and let pastern push,
but still we've caught
the wrong lead.

He feels the point;
language of bone, my weight
a tonal rift. Legs rip

common ground,
dig in and up.
Dialogue snag.
Balance no pliant victim,
the lead plays similar notes
as perfection.

Anatomical reverse,
we prescribe the where
and how of motion.
He sucks down
no formal protest.

Message bounced to sender:
left diagonal strums
obedience, touch whip to flank
re-beat the stance. *Where are*
you going? The source is silent

but written in motion.
Impulse is mine,
you share to survive,
leaning out.

Kind-eyed obedience
following a ruined track
of my own design,
every circle brings us back
to where we ought to be.

FICTIONS OF LEGS

Fear almost always arises – in horses as well as in
people – from concern about what might happen,
and much more rarely from what *is* happening.

—MARY WANLESS

Bodylines

Biological function is not opinion.

Opinion does not chart
muscles of
horse, deep and shallow
systemic tensors and cervical portions
serrate, or help bring
the hind when hoof
has landed, cartilages
preform spongy deposits
live to colonising ends
on bone, cavities
erupt, pad the thin bands
like sheepskin cloth
under saddle. Creasing contact,
knees close on their own
terms, not impatient ambition.
Enlarge and convert
according to
schedule,
seldom fitting with season,
show willing or best in hand,
hyaline cartilage all
that remains. Vessels
contract, legacy of time,
growth plates shown
but not labelled.

Draw Reins

Lever is set
term to tool
and back again,
a wiry tug
dropped head and
we will wear elegance
like a shroud.
Rider's hand,
a foam narrative –
chin on chest
mouth on throat –
that raspy carousel
grinds heels in
like a crank.
Intrusion zone
can hear the sounds,
press extinction
to the soles
of feet and mouth and
taste the flex
carrot stick strike –
mining honey
fat on ribs
for memory
of muscle under
friendly fire.
All conversation
one way.
Still, each horse will
gleam under wraps,
plumped for show.
Buyers lean in,
count strides
from stud
to slaughter.

Buyer Beware

You can't have perfect horses any more than you can have perfect men, or perfect women … those who've got horses to sell must lie.

—ANTHONY TROLLOPE

I'd rather be blind
than tie you in, pinioned
aesthetic – fetishising your frustration
as impulsion, energy, or spirit
to bend. To dominate or determine –
to leave you reeks
of stagnation, wastage absolved
in hands full of shrapnel.

Charmed circles around the priests
and rope-twirling testaments –
buy your prayers at the door,
lay-on-hands at clinics
or deliver online.
Cults of convenience,
sort of fictions: the oils
that keep us.

I've absorbed my share of spiels,
salesmen tied and smiling
at the rail. Peace and prosperity –
there is no discount for malice,
but it finds a way in at
the corners. Better be soft
than too remote, wrapped in a cult
of our long, old creation.

I bought your tongue and traumas,
your back and pad
of every botched move. Remove
the tags and take it on,
in this mess we're together.

Half-Pass

Our dialogue here is your stride
obedient under a fresh coat,
you step in and up, link and glide,
your mind remains remote.
Each gaze refined, a perfect transmission
no neater than speech would you find,
accept and receive every locution,
no touch of belly to remind.
Episodes of legs, I press for consent
and now, we slip from the path.
Though each tooth may clench with redder intent
you are wrapped too tightly from wrath:
we follow the lines, folding contours
trapped in the press of my spine to yours.

Slipped

For Gina's first, who didn't quite make it.

You opened the door
quite unplanned, access
sieging border of
intent. Heads lean
in, close ranks to take
the new addition. Your way
is clean as lines
across your family's
face, feeding their passage
too early for name.
Volcanic rise, smoke
now left ashen. *Rinjani.*
Each path is gifted
with shoulders that reach
and need. We welcome
even those not noticed.
And yet you've slipped away.
Now your act of entrance,
quiet and bewildered, is all the more
obscene for having left
unannounced. You sit in the hallway
of throats that bare and ache
for appellation. Bones turn
in sockets. Mouth will move
without a word. No more
the brace of waiting. Though none
have held you close, we all
must feel you go.

BY ANY OTHER NAME

Servant
Perhaps you have learn'd it without book:
But, I pray, can you read any thing you see?

Romeo
Ay, if I know the letters and the language.

Zebra

I

First morning, finding unfamiliar roads. Sole proprietor waiting around the curve, watched askance. Gravel crushed to path. We enter. Simulacrum holding court, I am caught. A familiar face in different clothes of the most striking sort, wade through cliché, but he speaks where I may not answer. Marginal hybrid, panels lean and untouchable, flick in familiar moves. Belly broad. One eye measures, another confirms. Lone stallion, I call on harem's edge or lion's gaze, waiting for some end. His lazy caution tips ear towards LandCruiser's grinding gaze, and pause. Not enough to hold us long. One equid body falls short of elephant bulk and rancour. The guide moves us on. But his vicious docility holds me firm. To speak transcends dialect, gives lines in the wrong hands. What he knows remains ahead, on ground where I have no right of passage. He won't move, so slowly side-step, vehicle slides on stones. For once I've to go without trying to start something. His gaze feeds until we are gone.

II

The next morning drive another appears, sad footnote on the way to bigger things. A band of three – two mares, one stallion – his fetlock ripe as crushed marula. His eye was not for us, but one mare he struck with both barrels, rapid fire leg suspended: spiteful gymnast makes a stand. Flagging the car, we watch as shoulders bear casualty onwards, lips crease with each halting step. Iron and copper rusting through. My first hand moves, but is quashed. Dismissal in a breath. A horse in need transcends all fences, but here, to rush in all hands and outrage, is fulsome rebuke. No right to life. At worst my move would send him on, to bolt would be to splinter, left hoof a soaked pennant. End the episode, leg a shattered frame. Cut past black, run the code. The other mare huffs down his neck; he moves towards the bush. He must not wilt within sight. Each suspects that stately walk will not have further to go, but its direction must never be our place.

III

The scrub settles to grey, no base for scale. Now, we spot your herd. A go-away bird swings over the cluster, but stays quiet. Hemmed by trees, hides smoked. They are standing nose to tail. Three soft bodies behind the lines, but no pause to snap your likeness: zebra aren't big sellers alive, after all. Guide has better targets to net. A clearer shot will come later, from the airport. I found you, by Departures, crisp bodies flat and shining under lights between the gates. Tufts and bristles. Hand slips over unfamiliar lines. Each skin pulled out, dried up, all soft elegance smashed, but so much easier to bear on arrival. Rugs and wraps. Here, it's not my place to gauge your pelt. Your fold is those who matter, each red-sun trail leading further away. I see no community. Those sad souvenirs and your calm silence here in the veldt. Back in Scotland, once they mounted skins on spears, pointing fortune forwards. Mouth open, propped for gifts. These bodies sprawl in wait. We are utterly outnumbered.

Przewalski's Pelts

These stone broad heads, mealy
fawn and striped, slip in
Chernobyl's exclusion zone.

Marginal equine, long
thought gone, clawed back
even now poachers outpace

recovery, gut and tan
hides remember aspic
comb and gunshot blush

firmer than bitted teeth.
Fringes stained, they skulk -
no sweeter than injustice

being named for the first
to claim your murder,
casting mane and tail

as though swearing away
sigils. In relief.
Evading taxonomy

each cream coat,
claims steppe and desert
beyond all.

The last stallion seen
in the Gobi sands,
alone for thirty years,

or patiently buried there,
waiting for new
herds to be spent.

Sable Island Horses

I am not an ocean narrative. My feet
are fingernail-soft, long hair and wide
gaze tangledrawn to shifting tides that rip
and rail against the sand.

Sea horse, island-bound my carousel
horizon draws shipwrecks, lung foam. Desperation
echoes, rebounds my own expulsion.

Sand and salt familiar, my tongue grows stern
on sea-grass. Thickening fog bars guests
who wring copper
or coal from our bodies.

Weedy morass, short-stumping this new-bred hide
grips all Atlantic spray. Pendent swings of ice
shies fetlocks upon the incline. Agency by exile.

We are our own.
Storm plains flex narrow dunes
to claim marrow. Cold bones sink to sea,
we need no hand to steer us
home.

Horse Latitudes

No red tide laps the shore
to mark your gory passage.
Algal bloom snuffs oxygen,
lungs filled in unfamiliar sea.

Cast adrift, no water to fill
your salted flanks:
they pitched you over the side
an empty barrel. Spanish soil

fell from your hooves
before Pacific
rose to claim
your abandoned hide.

Rolling atop the deep,
hawk head mauled
by foam. Sharks barter
your sinews
beneath calm water.

No horizon will beckon
you home, body
sunk – skull to mount
the bedrock, mapping
a legacy of bones.

Lake Gregory Horses

Do they know you're here?
How long has it been, this
time – off the truck or swam
ashore? You're not around
or from here, are you? They'll want
to check your pockets,
see your credentials if you
plan to stay, or else.
No pines to cloister
condemnation, here you're
soft and bare. Grass trees
and Kimberley casualties.
Wait in line or drown
where we can't see.
Safe and separate,
stationed and disbarred,
you've run from law.
There's a reason why
you aren't from here,
how you came
on boats.
You want a right to stay?
Not your call,
deed lines will be drawn
by the owners, not the tenants
who've made themselves at home,
just a little too late for comment.
All colours bleed brighter
behind wire lines.
Don't pay attention,
no signs for sale.
But do they hear the groans?
Each ruined body thrown to earth,
just out of cameras' lines, no dignity
in a lawnmower's spray.

Curriculum of silence,
better lost off shore.

And now
they want another trigger, another finger,
or for you to disappear:
for being named an entrant.
It's a little less fashionable
to remove people this way,
but give it time –
until that's all borrowed,
dug up on borrowed land.

No refuge
from redundancy, your mark
is vital, hooves slicing through
all. You have no place
among us,
unless you're fit
to work. Turn over all that is
precious, neat as a bullet through lungs.

JUSTICE FOR ROMEO

We call them dumb animals, and so they are,
for they cannot tell us how they feel,
but they do not suffer any less because they have no words.

—ANNA SEWELL

Treatment

is not singular. Different doses must be applied on trial or fully immersed. For me, removal. Node ungrown. Excise the fracture, sever scar tissue too dense to recover. Old growth, new depth. Taken away before more damage is done. Borderlines too wide, salted to sustain life. Had I the nerve, that loss would be the case. Splitting hairlines can rebuild nothing. It wasn't the ground that snapped me, but Romeo's back. Doctor confirms. No need for contact. The shock of eviction too much to handle. If I wait too long, my step will always hitch. Sudden shearing, a corner turned. He's gone where no one can follow. They won't sell them out those gates. Peace will come once the scarring settles, the doctor hopes. At least, there's a chance. *He's a bad one.* Pairing diagnoses – ruined backs both. Let you retire. I can't stop here, need to walk on. *No such thing.* Not all we miss is lost. Ill-fitted. Red horse matching stride for stride, getting further and further. We share scrutiny and the coldness of a door. I never saw it coming.

Fracture

I felt that rush
before I caught
the ground.

No settlement – arriving
on conquered ground
must always evoke
rejection.

But this was a slip. Suddenly
tectonic rift
in internal space.
Plates crack, contact.

Romeo rises,
and we both must come down.

Ally crept over,
intruder wears
familiar colours.

Clench fist recovery – rein always
under thumb, but now

hitch stride, lock eye
and release.

Denial has calmness
of iodine, waiting room peace
I am festering like a burn
behind wallpaper.

Romeo revised – a new home
in order, owner decides. Move along,
nothing to ignore.

Today, I'm remade
under lights –
hollow bones
on cold canvas –
watch the ceiling
set the scene.

Romeo ruptures,
hill rose and fell
out of sight.

What border grows
this time?

How deep
will we find
the stray loop,
snapped stitch,
line cast in error?

To see is not to hold,
mirror gridlocks me down,
measure fault and drop
in sections,
dust-sheeted and dry-eyed
beneath the camera.

Romeo remote. I am rewritten
in scripts.

Cold toes clench on plate,
all protests behind closed eyes.

Spine diverted – Romeo shamed –
now both must take another route.

Theory for Everything and Nothing

Somehow I'd forgotten
that Romeo always dies in the end.

I know why,
but can't set it.

Threads link
teeth and tones,
find the space
down where
you are pieces.

I thought we'd agreed
to let him go –
dichotic connection
always meant to shear.
Half an hourglass
can turn
either way.

Shot on the sly.
Phone lay
silent until evening.
Morning wasted
on a call waiting.
They didn't even save me his tail.
No pieces to gather, only character
limits of online memorials.
Space for another to fill,
fed mouths.
Romeo exits.

Copper of abattoir funerals
wrings our throats.
All knots,
lines toed in and one tooth gone,
he's lost his name
to meat truck madness –
two days to drain him.

So that's that.
Stormy to Jerry
to Romeo. No names
to call, no hand at your head
when the bell came.

I don't know
when they did it – but the theory's here,
blood cast on the floor
an off-screen fact
sluice freed.
All your fragments, still
and criminal, hands
caught. I take my place in that final scene,
letting you down one last time.

IN MEMORIAM

A horse can lend its rider the speed and strength
he or she lacks, but the rider who is wise
remembers it is no more than a loan.

—PAM BROWN

Sold On

Wasn't my idea,
you've carried the weight
all the same. Now, at last,
I see you again. You are ceded

territory – beloved space
a skin of cartography
flecked with age.
White rusts through
your hair, knees crevasse
where you slipped
off-screen, a footnote
I read later, up in Cambridge.

You traversed the coastal plain,
sent south. Augustan ticks burned
joints, fluid seeping
into each valley. Now fallow, you own
these fields where I watch
my step for snakes.

This time when we meet, no
rein feeds my current to you,
a resolute republic. I touch
the borders, draw glance,
and step back.
There are places

I could send your hair, lock
you between pearls upon my wrist,
for memory's sake.
I palm your tail,
each tress a fingerprint.
It took years to grow
but only seconds to sever.

Rinjani

Comma splash
quotation, as if
en-dash were not
enough. Already
you were an act
of communication.

But this was no greeting,
only intermission.
Your tongue, flat and soft,
took my fingers.
New ridges familiar against all
common sense. You took

my taste and turned each
whisker over arm, face,
neck. You knew
each join as your mother
watched. Taking my hand
you left the smallest print,

but I may touch
on your terms only.
No treaty here.
You were pathways
and furrows that should have burst
and grown past me with every visit.

I am left on the side
of the fence with your mother,
the same that took your back
in two. Watchers on the lines
cannot dare to question
why you came and quickly left.

For Gina

Finger crooked, your reply
will always slant my words.

Finding prints, or passage.

Dark horse hardwired
to encroaching wind,

an object to crave

wearing penance of circles
to breach another's gap.

Now, read the body.

We learned lines
to repeat on rote,

head stooped to steer

I would break that finger
myself to take that line

from crude patter, then

we'd steal anything, fantastic
and askew, each revelation

still more side-long

than the last. Half-
thoughts delivered,

we close the loops,

and touch is still transgression.

Our surreal silence

Each step will be replayed -
widower at the gate

this, at least,

is a conceit only I will
have to carry.

You have been here
in every twist.

Each page for you
if not in kind, at least

in reason.

I would not presume
to write your reply

nor follow after

but I love you more now
than I ever have in my whole life.

NOTES

Quotations appearing throughout the text are taken from the following sources:

page 5: Alois Podhajsky, *The Riding Teacher*, London: The Sportsman's Press, 1993.

page 5: Robert Smith Surtees, *Mr Sponge's Sporting Tour*, New York: Stringer & Townsend, 1856.

page 16: Mary B Moore, 'Horse Care as Depicted on Greek Vases before 400 B.C.', *Metropolitan Museum Journal* (1.39, 2004): pp. 8, 35–67.

page 24: The Arabian Horse Society Ltd. of Australia, 'Regulations as of 1st January, 2015': http://ahsa.asn.au/forms.html

page 26: John Cage, quoted in David Revill, *The Roaring Silence*, New York: Arcade, 1992.

page 41: D Bixvy-Hammett & WH Brooks, 'Common Injuries in Horseback Riding. A Review', Sports Medicine, (9.1, January 1990), pp. 36–47.

page 44: Alison Harman, interview with Jonica Newby, 'Riding Blind', *Catalyst*, ABC Television, 2 May 2002: http://www.abc.net.au/catalyst/stories/s545781.htm

page 51: Anthony Trollope, *Can You Forgive Her?*, ed. Dinah Birch, Oxford: Oxford University Press, 2012.

page 65: Anna Sewell, *Black Beauty*, London: Jarrold & Sons, 1877.

ACKNOWLEDGEMENTS

Poems in this collection first appeared in *Avatar Review*, *Contrapasso Magazine*, *Cordite Poetry Review*, *Page Seventeen*, *Plumwood Mountain*, *Rabbit* and *Writ Review*.

My sincere thanks to everyone who has helped with this collection, especially Kent MacCarter, Rosalind McFarlane, Matthew Hall and John Kinsella for their feedback and tireless support at all stages. Thank you as well to my family, particularly Kyle, for listening to each part of the collection as it grew and adapted, and to Dennis Haskell for his introduction.

Though the horses care very little, this book would not have been possible without their teachings. My thanks go to Gina, Rinjani, River, Romeo and Saddiq.

This project has been assisted by the Australian Government through the Australia Council, its arts funding and advisory body.

Australian Government | Australia Council for the Arts

Siobhan Hodge has a PhD in English literature from The University of Western Australia. Her thesis focused on Sappho's legacy in English translations. Her chapbook of reflections on Sappho, *Picking up the Pieces*, was published in 2012 as part of the Wide Range Chapbooks series. Hodge is currently the reviews editor for *Writ Review* and a contributing reviewer for *Cordite Poetry Review*. She is also an associate editor for *Rochford Street Review*, and was previously a project officer for Trove. She was the winner of the Patricia Hackett Poetry Prize in 2015, and has had creative and critical works published in *Axon: Creative Explorations*, *Peril* and *Westerly*. She divides her time between Hong Kong and Australia, and has nurtured an obsession with horses for most of her life.